This book belongs to

_____

To Linda and Paul,
who have instilled in me the wonder of infinite
possibility alongside the north star
of self-compassion.

To Elizabeth,
whose brilliance and generous spirit shines
ever-brightly through the inevitable gray clouds
overhead.

To Rebecca and Ezra,
our origins have forged an unbreakable bond
of love and mutual respect.

To Noah, Avi, Ella, and children everywhere,
may you read these words and remember that
you belong, have inner reserves beyond your
imagination, and are always enough.

www.mascotbooks.com

You've Always Been Good Enough

For more information, please contact:
Mascot Kids, an imprint of Amplify Publishing Group
620 Herndon Parkway #220
Herndon, VA 20170
info@mascotbooks.com

CPSIA Code: PRKF0323A
Library of Congress Control Number: 2022915499
ISBN-13: 978-1-63755-277-3

Printed in China

You've Always Been Good Enough

Jonah Cohen, MD

Illustrated by
Margaret Jane Sullivan

You've always been good enough,
and you always will be.

Nothing can change your worth to me.

You're good enough as you are,
born underneath the stars.

Neither great heights nor deep
depths can change who you are.

It is not because of what you do,
what you create, or even your name.

Your worth is unchangeable, precious all the same.

There's no need to compare to others,
as this is surely a trap.

For envy or pride can find you lost on your map.

There are times when you may stumble,
times when life will fray.

Be gentle with yourself
as you find your way.

There's no room for regret,
there are things we cannot change.

Try to love this moment,
even when it feels strange.

Your true gold
is within,
shining bright
from inside out.

Neither rags
nor riches can change
what you're about.

You are constantly unfolding,
growing by the day.

Keep gratitude in your heart—
it won't lead you astray.

Treat your body like a temple,
for it's the only one you've got.

Eat fruits and veggies, get your rest,
and move around a lot.

Strive for moderation
and follow the golden mean.

Instead of a tightrope, try walking
a nice, wide balance beam.

Be kind to others,
for you never know their lot.

Everyone hurts and everyone
loves—remember this thought.

Treasure our precious green planet,
snow and sun, cold and hot.

Look after Mother Earth—
she's the only one we've got.

And when you find gray clouds over head,
when that voice in your mind says you've failed,
remember these simple words from your heart
and you'll be sure to prevail.

You've always been good enough,
and you always will be.

Nothing can change your worth to me.

ABOUT THE AUTHOR

Jonah Cohen is a physician at Harvard Medical School. Born in Upstate New York, he attended Brown University for college and medical school. He is also a visual artist and singer-songwriter. *You've Always Been Good Enough* is his debut children's book, inspired by his family. He lives in Massachusetts with his wife and their three children.